How to Be Healthy!

Go Wash Up

Keeping Clean

by Amanda Doering Tourville   illustrated by Ronnie Rooney

PiCTURE WiNDOW BOOKS
Minneapolis, Minnesota

Special thanks to our advisers for their expertise:

Nora L. Howley, M.A., School Health Consultant
Silver Spring, Maryland

Terry Flaherty, Ph.D., Professor of English
Minnesota State University, Mankato

Editor: Christianne Jones
Designer: Tracy Davies
Page Production: Michelle Biedscheid
Art Director: Nathan Gassman
The illustrations in this book were created with
ink and watercolor.

Picture Window Books are published by Capstone.
1710 Roe Crest Drive, North Mankato, Minnesota 56003
www.capstonepub.com

Printed in the United States of America in North Mankato, Minnesota.
102012   007004

Library of Congress Cataloging-in-Publication Data
Tourville, Amanda Doering, 1980–
Go wash up : keeping clean / by Amanda Doering Tourville;
illustrated by Ronnie Rooney.
p. cm. — (How to be healthy!)
Includes index.
ISBN 978-1-4048-4808-5 (library binding)
ISBN 978-1-4795-2025-1 (ss pbk)
1. Hygiene—Juvenile literature. I. Rooney, Ronnie. II. Title.
RA777.T68 2009
613'.4—dc22   2008006418

Keeping your body clean is important. It helps you stay healthy. Washing your body removes dirt and germs that make you sick. There are many ways to keep clean.

Owen washes his hands before he eats.
He washes with soap and warm water.

Before every meal, wash your hands with soap and warm water for at least 20 seconds.

Owen's dad helps him cut his fingernails. Owen uses a special brush to clean under his nails.

Dirt and germs can get under your fingernails.
Trimming your nails helps keep them clean.

7

Owen washes his whole body in the bath. He puts soap on a washcloth and scrubs from top to bottom.

Make sure to wash behind your ears and under your arms.

Owen washes his hair with shampoo.

He rinses his hair with clean water until all of the shampoo is out.

Everyone's hair is different. You might need to wash your hair every day. You might need to wash your hair only once a week.

In the morning, Owen washes his face with soap.

When washing your face, make sure not to get soap in your eyes. Soap will make your eyes sting.

After washing, he dries his face with a clean towel.

Owen brushes his teeth after breakfast.
He brushes for two minutes. Then he flosses.

Brushing cleans your teeth and
makes your breath smell nice. You
should brush at least twice a day.

Owen puts on clean clothes every day. He wears clean socks, clean underwear, and a clean T-shirt.

16

Part of keeping clean is wearing clean clothes. Dirty clothes can make your body dirty, too.

17

Achoo! Owen sneezes into a tissue. Using a tissue when he sneezes keeps germs from getting on his hands.

Don't sneeze into your hands. Instead, sneeze into the inside of your elbow if you don't have a tissue.

Owen brushes his hair every day. He gets his hair cut every six weeks.

To prevent spreading head lice, do not share combs, brushes, or hats with friends.

While bathing, make sure to clean between your toes and under your toenails.

22

In the summer, Owen washes his feet after he plays outside. This keeps his feet clean. It also keeps dirt and germs out of his house. Owen keeps clean and stays healthy.

To Learn More

More Books to Read

Gordon, Sharon. *Keeping Clean.* New York: Children's Press, 2002.

Salzmann, Mary Elizabeth. *Keeping Your Body Clean.* Edina, Minn.: Abdo, 2004.

Spilsbury, Louise. *Why Should I Wash My Body?: and Other Questions About Keeping Clean and Healthy.* Chicago: Heinemann Library, 2003.

On the Web

FactHound offers a safe, fun way to find Web sites related to topics in this book. All of the sites on FactHound have been researched by our staff.

1. Visit *www.facthound.com*
2. Type in this special code: 1404848088
3. Click on the FETCH IT button.

Your trusty FactHound will fetch the best sites for you!

Look for all of the books in the How to Be Healthy! series:

Brush, Floss, and Rinse: Caring for Your Teeth and Gums
Fuel the Body: Eating Well
Get Up and Go: Being Active
Go Wash Up: Keeping Clean

Index